FRED J. SCHONELL
THE ESSENTIAL SPELLING BOOK 2

W0006288

9780174240822

Nelson

Gregory Mankin

A very good start Gregory.
well done!

laugh	lately	motor	lonely
laughed	safely	visitor	likely
laughter	nicely	victory	likeness
linger	lovely	inform	weakness

☆ Learn the words, then use them to do the exercises.

☆ **WORD PUZZLE** Use words from the list to complete the puzzle.

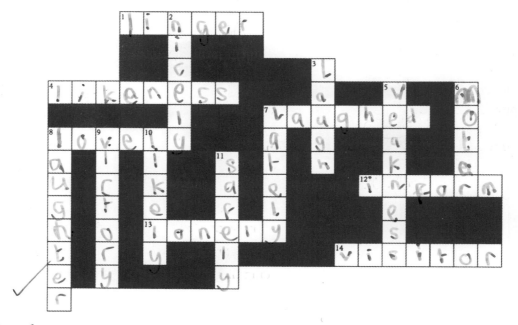

Clues down

2 pleasantly
3 express mirth
5 a failing
6 automobile
7 recently
8 expression of mirth
9 triumph
10 probable
11 not dangerously

Clues across

1 delay departure
4 similarity
7 expressed mirth
8 beautiful
12 to tell
13 without companions
14 caller

☆ **WORD HUNT** Which words in the list have these smaller words inside them?

1 one __lonely__
2 ice __nicely__
3 for __inform__
4 ate __lately__

☆ **WORD MAKER** Use words from the list to complete the words below.

1 __lone__ ly (solitary)
2 __like__ ly (possible)
3 __love__ ly (beautiful)
4 __late__ ly (recently)

servant	though	arrive	constant
merchant	through	advice	admit
distant	empire	adventure	amuse
important	admire	nature	ashamed

☆ Learn the words, then use them to do the exercises.

☆ **OPPOSITES**   Find words in the list which mean the opposite of these words.

1 near _____distant_____   5 depart _____arrive_____

2 trivial _____important_____   6 proud _____ashamed_____

3 fickle _____constant_____   7 deny _____admit_____

4 despise _____admire_____

☆ **WORD PUZZLE**   Use the word 'important' to help form nine words from the list.

1 a	d	v	i	c	e				
	2 a	m	u	s	e				
	3 e	m	p	i	r	e			
	4 t	h	o	u	g	h			
	5 t	h	r	o	u	g	h		
	6 m	a	t	u	r	e			
7 m	e	r	c	h	a	n	t		
	8 a	d	v	e	n	t	u	r	e
9 s	e	r	v	a	n	t			

counsel

entertain

many territories under one ruler

despite the fact that

going in at one side and out at the other

a wild, primitive state

a buyer and seller of goods

a risky undertaking

one paid to do household duties

☆ **WORD HUNT**   Complete these sentences with words from the list.

1 The word with the same letters as 'taverns' is _____servant_____.

2 The word with the most vowels is _____adventure_____.

3 The word with only two consonants is _____amused_____.

4 Something which is far away is _____distant_____.

5 When you do something wrong you feel _____ashamed_____.   ashamed

6 An _____adventure_____ is an exciting event.

7 When something doesn't change, it is _____constant_____.

evening	object	sailor	rough
event	subject	tailor	tough
equator	robin	railway	rainy
enough	holiday	daily	rocky

☆ Learn the words, then use them to do the exercises.

☆ **WORD HUNT** Fill the gaps in the poem with words from the list.

Jones and Chaney

Captain Jones, a former (1) _sailor_ ,

And Thomas Chaney, village (2) _tailor_ ,

Decided they would go away

And book themselves a (3) _Holiday_ .

Their (4) _event_ was to find a crater   object

On a mountain high on the (5) _equator_ .

The seas were (6) _rough_ , the weather (7) _rainy_ .

The second (8) _evening_ Jones said, "Chaney,

Conditions here are pretty (9) _tough_ .

Believe me, friend, I've had (10) _enough_ .

Why don't we go to the (11) _railway_ station

And find another destination?"

"I quite agree," Tom Chaney said.

They went to Canada instead

And found a place where many fountains

Poured headlong down the (12) _Rocky_ Mountains.

They went out fishing three times (13) _daily_

And caught big salmon, fresh and scaly.

Each night occurred the same (14) _Subject_ .   (event)

A (15) _robin_ sang just by their tent.

Until they gave him from their dish

His nightly piece of tasty fish.

Now Canada is in their blood.

They won't come home. They're there for good!

sparrow	village	ought	thought
swallow	cabbage	bought	ragged
valley	carrot	brought	scatter
valleys	gallop	fought	brass

☆ Learn the words, then use them to do the exercises.

☆ **WORD HUNT**   Which words in the list have these smaller words inside them?

1 car _carrot_

2 ill _village_

3 row _sparrow_

4 cat _scatter_

5 cab _cabbage_

6 wall _swallow_

7 alleys _valleys_

8 rag _ragged_

9 thou _thought_

☆ **WORD PUZZLE**   Use the word 'brought' to help make seven words from the list.

		b	o	u	g	h	t	purchased
	b	r	a	s	s			metal made from copper and zinc
g	a	l	l	o	p			fast ride on a horse
	f	o	u	g	h	t		struggled against
v	i	l	l	a	g	e		small country community
		r	h	o	u	g	h	t	believed
o	u	g	h	t				express duty or obligation

☆ **EXPLANATIONS**   Complete these sentences with words from the list.

1 The word which means 'conveyed' is _brought_.

2 Another word for 'spread' is _scatter_.

3 Another word for 'struggled' or 'quarrelled' is _fought_.

4 A _valley_ is a low stretch of land between hills.

☆ **WORD HUNT**   Complete these sentences with words from the list.

1 There was a _ragged_ tear in the curtain.

2 I polished the _brass_ candlestick.

3 The horse took off at a _gallop_.

alone	nasty	vanish	fancy
across	hasty	banish	ugly
among	shady	perish	polish
against	study	parish	Welsh

☆ Learn the words, then use them to do the exercises.

☆ **WORD PUZZLE** Use words from the list to complete the puzzle.

Clues down
1 opposed to
2 hurried
4 unpleasant
5 area served by a church
6 ornamented
9 expel
11 of unpleasant appearance

Clues across
1 from one side to the other
3 solitary
7 in the midst of
8 full of shade
10 look at closely
12 disappear
13 belonging to Wales
14 to make shiny

☆ **WORD MATCH** Find words in the list which mean the same as these words.

1 disappear _____

2 exile _____

3 die _____

4 quick _____

5 horrible _____

6 amidst _____

☆ **OPPOSITES** Find words in the list which mean the opposite of these words.

1 slow _____

2 for _____

3 appear _____

4 plain _____

lawn	lays	beauty	faithfully
dawn	laying	beautiful	welcome
famous	laid	careful	until
dangerous	thankful	carefully	unable

☆ Learn the words, then use them to do the exercises.

☆ **WORD HUNT**   Which words in the list have these smaller words inside them?

1 am _famous_

2 come _welcome_

3 law _lawn_

4 anger _dangerous_

5 it _faithfully_

6 aid _laid_

☆ **WORD PUZZLE**   Use the word 'unable' to help form six words from the list.

¹u	n	a	b	l	e		not possible to do
²u	n	t	i	l			up to
³l	a	y	s				puts down
	⁴b	e	a	u	t	y	loveliness
	⁵l	a	y	i	n	g	putting down
⁶w	e	l	c	o	m	e	gladly receive

☆ **OPPOSITES**   Find words in the list which mean the opposite of these words.

1 sunset _dawn_

2 ugly _beautiful_

3 ungrateful _thankful_

4 careless _careful_

5 carelessly _carefully_

6 safe _dangerous_

☆ **WORD MATCH**   Find words in the list which mean the same as these words.

1 lovely _beautiful_

2 renowned _famous_

3 loyally _faithfully_

glance	protect	stumble	scramble
advance	monster	grumble	bundle
distance	bough	thimble	kindle
France	plough	tremble	noble

☆ Learn the words, then use them to do the exercises.

☆ **WORD MAKER**   Use words from the list to complete the words below.

1   _ _ _ le   (showing high character or qualities)

2   _ _ _ _ le   (to light)

3   _ _ _ _ _ le   (to complain)

4   _ _ _ _ _ le   (to shake)

☆ **WORD HUNT**   Which words in the list have these smaller words inside them?

1	rot	_____	7	kind	_____
2	on	_____	8	tumble	_____
3	lance	_____	9	van	_____
4	him	_____	10	ran	_____
5	bun	_____	11	rumble	_____
6	ramble	_____	12	tan	_____

☆ **WORD PUZZLE**   Use words from the list to complete the puzzle.

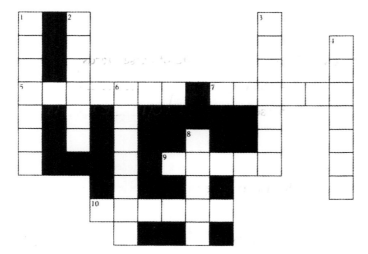

Clues down
1   trip
2   a hasty look
3   go forward
4   shake
6   cap for finger when sewing
8   main branch of a tree

Clues across
5   inhuman person
7   land of the French
9   dignified
10   agricultural implement

tight	bucket	error	Scottish
slight	trumpet	terror	mutton
delight	shrub	ribbon	blossom
mighty	liberty	cotton	correct

☆ Learn the words, then use them to do the exercises.

☆ **WORD PUZZLE**   Use words from the list to complete the puzzle.

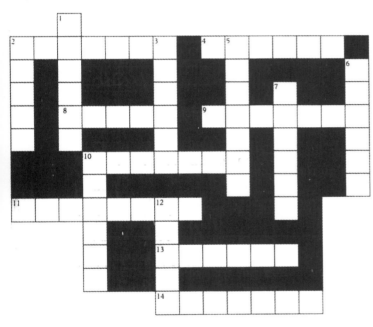

Clues down
1 pail
2 closed firmly
3 great fear
5 freedom
6 flesh of sheep
7 strong
10 fibre used to make cloth
12 woody bush

Clues across
2 brass musical instrument
4 trivial
8 mistake
9 great pleasure
10 right
11 belonging to Scotland
13 narrow strip of material
14 bloom

☆ **OPPOSITES**   Find words in the list which mean the opposite of these words.

1 slack _____

2 weak _____

3 wrong _____

4 slavery _____

5 serious _____

☆ **WORD MATCH**   Find words in the list which mean the same as these words.

1 pleasure _____

2 freedom _____

3 fear _____

4 mistake _____

chalk	gaze	discover	size
stalk	blaze	distinct	prize
salt	razor	discuss	dislike
alter	lazy	distress	disgrace

☆ Learn the words, then use them to do the exercises.

☆ **WORD PUZZLE**   Use the word 'distress' to help make eight words from the list.

	d							to find disagreeable
2	i							talk about
3	s							learn about for the first time
4	t							stem
5	r							shaving implement
6	e							a fixed look
7	s							clear
8	s							shame

☆ **WORD MAKER**   Use words from the list to complete the words below.

1 _ al _   (used to flavour food)

2 _ _ al _   (soft, white limestone)

3 al _ _ _   (to change)

4 _ _ _ ze   (bright flame)

5 _ _ _ ze   (a reward for success)

6 _ _ ze   (dimension)

☆ **OPPOSITES**   Find words in the list which mean the opposite of these words.

1 energetic   _____

2 lose   _____

3 well-being _____

4 hazy   _____

nation	company	rubber	question
station	companion	bullet	appear
dictation	astonish	quarrel	quart
motion	publish	barrel	quarter

☆ Learn the words, then use them to do the exercises.

☆ **WORD PUZZLE**   Use words from the list to complete the puzzle.

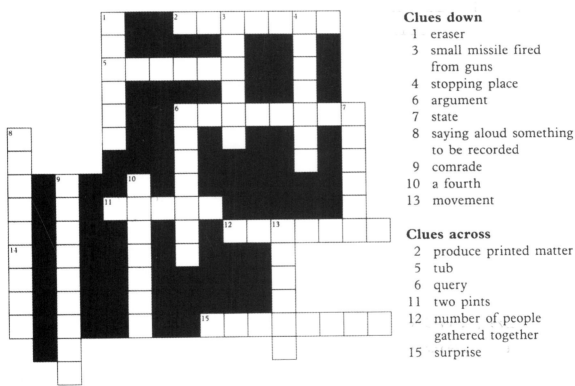

Clues down

1 eraser
3 small missile fired from guns
4 stopping place
6 argument
7 state
8 saying aloud something to be recorded
9 comrade
10 a fourth
13 movement

Clues across

2 produce printed matter
5 tub
6 query
11 two pints
12 number of people gathered together
15 surprise

☆ **WORD HUNT**   Complete these sentences with words from the list.

1 The word of which 'pea' is a part is _____.

2 The word of which 'ton' is a part is _____.

3 The word of which 'let' is a part is _____.

horrid	**belief**	**wharf**	**occupy**
coffee	**believe**	**wharves**	**hollow**
occur	**grieve**	**niece**	**forgotten**
occurred	**ourselves**	**piece**	**combine**

☆ Learn the words, then use them to do the exercises.

☆ **WORD HUNT** Which words in the list have these smaller words inside them?

1 cup _____

2 low _____

3 bin _____

4 off _____

5 pie _____

6 elves _____

☆ **WORD PUZZLE** Use words from the list to complete the puzzle.

Clues down
2 happened
3 dock
5 plural of 3 down
6 to live in
7 daughter of your sister
8 feel great sorrow
12 opinion

Clues across
1 not solid
4 unpleasant
6 happen
9 plural of 'myself'
10 bit
11 join together
13 accept as true
14 not remembered

caught	**stir**	**knit**	**office**
taught	**stirred**	**knitting**	**officer**
daughter	**mirror**	**knight**	**different**
naughty	**bonnet**	**skill**	**skirt**

☆ Learn the words, then use them to do the exercises.

☆ **WORD HUNT**   Fill in the gaps in the story with words from the list.

Mrs Smith is a woman police (1) _____. When she is not busy in the

(2) _____ she loves to (3) _____. She makes lots of

(4) _____ clothes. Last month she made a (5) _____ and a

(6) _____ to match. She put them on and looked at herself in the

(7) _____. She was very pleased with her (8) _____.

☆ **WORD MAKER**   Use words from the list to complete the words below.

1 _ augh _   (trapped)

2 _ augh _   (gave instruction to)

3 _ augh _ _ _   (girl child)

4 _ augh _ _   (badly behaved)

5 _ _ ir   (move around)

6 _ _ ir _   (female clothing)

7 _ ir _ _ _   (looking glass)

☆ **WORD HUNT**   Which words in the list have these smaller words inside them?

1 net   _____

2 red   _____

3 ill   _____

4 rent   _____

5 night _____

potato	value	instead	foe
potatoes	continue	steadily	poetry
tomato	statue	weary	butcher
tomatoes	thread	wearily	shilling

☆ Learn the words, then use them to do the exercises.

☆ **WORD PUZZLE**   Use words from the list to complete the puzzle.

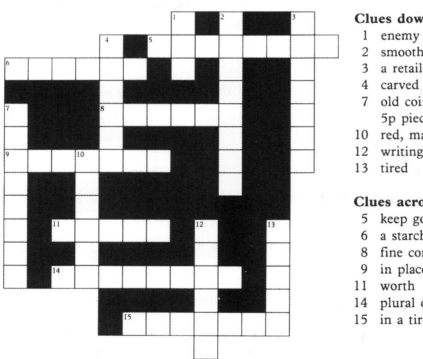

Clues down

1 enemy
2 smoothly
3 a retailer of meat
4 carved figure
7 old coin replaced by the 5p piece
10 red, many seeded fruit
12 writing in verse
13 tired

Clues across

5 keep going
6 a starchy root vegetable
8 fine cord of twisted fibre
9 in place of
11 worth
14 plural of 6 across
15 in a tired manner

☆ **WORD HUNT**   Complete these sentences with words from the list.

1 My brother made a lovely salad with lettuce and red _____.

2 The _____ of Liberty is in the USA.

3 Give me a needle and _____ and I'll darn it.

tunnel	pleasant	groan	defeat
suppose	pleasure	coach	tiger
cunning	measure	toast	reward
muddy	treasure	throat	shoe

☆ Learn the words, then use them to do the exercises.

☆ **WORD HUNT**   Fill in the story with words from the list.

A Clever Prince

A (1) _____ had grown too old to hunt but he had not lost his

(2) _____. He let it be known that there was a great (3) _____

hidden in the (4) _____ where he had his den. The entrance was very

(5) _____. Many treasure seekers got stuck in the mud and were eaten by the

beast.

The king decided to offer a (6) _____ to the one who killed the beast.

His own son said, "I (7) _____ a prince should show an example. It will give

me great (8) _____ to slay this beast."

The prince pretended to be stuck in the mud. Seeing this, the animal thought, "What a

(9) _____ surprise! Another easy dinner for me." He opened his jaws to seize

the prince. But the prince, who had taken off a (10) _____, rammed it down

the creature's (11) _____. The animal gave a loud (12) _____

and choked to death.

The king had watched the creature's (13) _____ from the royal

(14) _____. Pouring out a (15) _____ of wine he said, "Let us

drink a (16) _____ to my brave son. From now on he shall rule in my place."

And so he did, and wisely too, for many a long day.

☆ **WORD MATCH**   Find words in the list which mean the same as these words.

1 sly   _____

2 delight   _____

3 beat   _____

4 nice   _____

obey	dwelling	group	prettier
obeyed	wedding	wound	prettiest
swept	herring	youth	beginning
crept	vessel	calm	journey

☆ Learn the words, then use them to do the exercises.

☆ **WORD HUNT**   Which words in the list have these smaller words inside them?

1 tie _____

2 din _____

3 ring _____

4 urn _____

5 well _____

6 beg _____

7 wept _____

8 be _____

9 up _____

10 you _____

☆ **WORD PUZZLE**   Use the word 'beginning' to help form nine words from the list.

b	carry out orders
e	ship or container
g	small band
i	more pretty
n	place of residence
n	marriage ceremony
i	most pretty of all
n	trip or voyage
g	fish with large silvery scales

☆ **WORD HUNT**   Complete these sentences with words from the list.

1 The _____ was deep but the doctor said it didn't need stitches.

2 We decided to swim because the sea was so _____.

3 The cat _____ up on the mouse and pounced on it.

recall	demand	feather	health
result	deliver	leather	healthy
beyond	depend	weather	wealthy
shiver	delay	breath	meant

☆ Learn the words, then use them to do the exercises.

☆ **STEP WORDS**   Use words from the list to complete the puzzle.

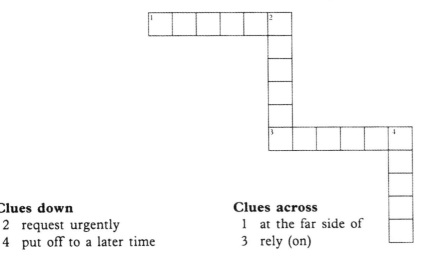

Clues down
2 request urgently
4 put off to a later time

Clues across
1 at the far side of
3 rely (on)

☆ **WORD MAKER**   Use words from the list to complete the words below.

1 __ __ ea __ __   (air drawn in by the lungs)

2 __ ea __ __ __ __   (skin of animals)

3 __ ea __ __ __ __   (degree of warmth or coldness)

4 __ ea __ __ __ __   (growth on body of bird)

5 __ ea __ __ __ __   (sound in body)

6 __ ea __ __ __ __   (rich)

☆ **EXPLANATIONS**   Complete these sentences with words from the list.

1 Another word for 'remember' is _____.

2 Another word for 'tremble' is _____.

3 Another word for 'consequence' is _____.

4 'Physical state' means _____.

5 Another word for 'intended' is _____.

fleet	**drown**	**aim**	**deer**
screen	**drowned**	**claim**	**steer**
greedy	**powder**	**praise**	**queer**
freedom	**petrol**	**dairy**	**engage**

☆ Learn the words, then use them to do the exercises.

☆ **WORD PUZZLE**   Use words from the list to complete the puzzle.

Clues down

1 odd
2 guide
4 gluttonous
5 dust or tiny loose particles
7 a frame to conceal something
8 killed by immersion in liquid
9 intention
10 fuel for motor engines

Clues across

3 employ
6 commend
8 animals with antlers
11 liberty
12 store room for milk and cream
13 kill by immersion in water
14 quick
15 a demand for payment

☆ **WORD MATCH**   Find words in the list which mean the same as these words.

1 shelter _____

2 peculiar _____

3 liberty _____

4 employ _____

5 avaricious _____

6 direct towards _____

guilty	season	medal	Briton
guide	reason	metal	British
guest	crimson	mental	Irish
warn	iron	board	Ireland

☆ Learn the words, then use them to do the exercises.

☆ **WORD PUZZLE**   Use the word 'Ireland' to help form seven words from the list.

belonging to Britain

belonging to Ireland

a period of the year

responsible for an offence

cause

deep red

long thin piece of sawn timber

☆ **WORD HUNT**   Which words in the list have these smaller words inside them?

1 ton _____

2 war _____

3 and _____

4 rim _____

5 met _____

6 oar _____

7 men _____

8 on _____

☆ **WORD MAKER**   Use words from the list to complete the words below.

1 _ _ _ al   (metal disc often given as award)

2 _ _ _ _ al   (of the mind)

3 gu _ _ _   (one who shows the way)

4 gu _ _ _   (person who gets hospitality)

5 _ _ _ _ on   (Autumn is one)

6 _ _ _ _ _ on   (a colour)

7 _ _ on   (a kind of metal)

relate	desire	bathe	December
retire	deserve	vase	October
restore	behave	rare	Germany
refuse	bravery	square	herd

☆ Learn the words, then use them to do the exercises.

☆ **WORD PUZZLE**   Use words from the list to complete the puzzle.

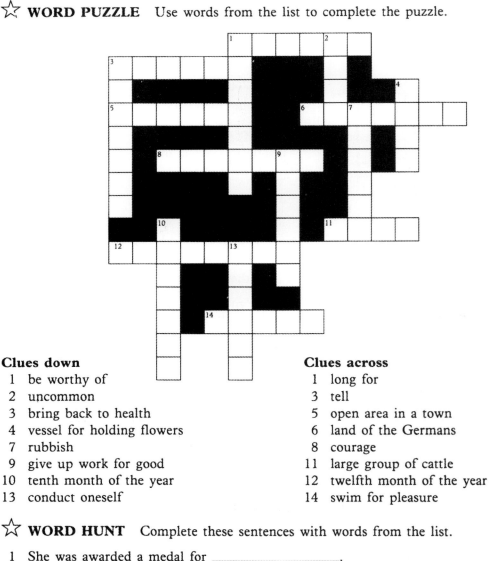

Clues down
1 be worthy of
2 uncommon
3 bring back to health
4 vessel for holding flowers
7 rubbish
9 give up work for good
10 tenth month of the year
13 conduct oneself

Clues across
1 long for
3 tell
5 open area in a town
6 land of the Germans
8 courage
11 large group of cattle
12 twelfth month of the year
14 swim for pleasure

☆ **WORD HUNT**   Complete these sentences with words from the list.

1 She was awarded a medal for _____.

2 There was a _____ of cattle in the field.

3 My parents are going to _____ to Spain.

attend	edge	flour	lodge
attack	hedge	sour	bridge
wreck	badge	trout	sword
wrong	judge	stout	check

☆ Learn the words, then use them to do the exercises.

☆ **WORD PUZZLE**   Use words from the list to complete the puzzle.

Clues down

1 destroy
2 a boundary or shrubs
3 decide upon a case
6 examine

Clues across

4 be present at
5 launch an assault
7 margin
8 emblem

☆ **OPPOSITES**   Find words in the list which mean the opposite of these words.

1 right _____

2 defend _____

3 slim _____

4 sweet _____

☆ **WORD HUNT**   Complete these sentences with words from the list.

1 The _____ over the river was unsafe.

2 I caught a large _____ in the river and cooked it for dinner.

3 My sister forgot to put the _____ in the cake.

4 The _____ in the grounds of the big house was up for sale.

5 The _____ fight in the film was very exciting.

suit	member	wore	bowl
fruit	remember	score	factory
orange	remembered	whom	basement
banana	memory	weather	pavement

☆ Learn the words, then use them to do the exercises.

☆ **MINI PUZZLE**   Use words from the list to complete the puzzle.

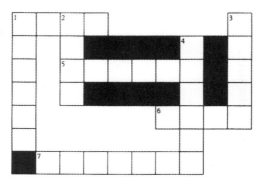

Clues down

1 a yellow fruit
2 word used at times instead of 'who'
3 twenty
4 ability of the brain to remember

Clues across

1 round, open container
5 a citrus fruit
6 deteriorated from constant use
7 building where goods are manufactured

☆ **WORD MAKER**   Use words from the list to complete the words below.

1 _ _ _ _ _ ment   (sidewalk)

2 _ _ _ _ ment   (cellar)

3 _ ui _   (set of garments)

4 _ _ ui _   (edible part of a plant)

☆ **WORD HUNT**   Complete these sentences with words from the list.

1 The word _____ is part of two other words in the list

2 Another word for 'recall' is _____.

3 Another word for 'climate' is _____.

4 The word which contains 'e' four times is _____.

using	eight	figure	pour
during	weight	scripture	court
duty	weigh	creature	shoulder
truth	dumb	entertain	huge

☆ Learn the words, then use them to do the exercises.

☆ **WORD PUZZLE**   Use words from the list to complete the puzzle.

Clues down

1 very big
2 a proven fact
3 a sacred book
5 a task that one feels bound to perform
6 a living being
7 human form

Clues across

3 where the arm joins the body
4 cause to flow in a stream
5 unable to speak
6 a king's household
8 making use of
9 for the duration of

☆ **WORD HUNT**   Complete these sentences with words from the list.

1 The child has been deaf and _____ since birth.

2 Four and four make _____.

3 The boxer had to _____ in before the fight.

4 We had some drinks _____ the interval.

5 The box was a terrible _____ and I couldn't lift it.

6 The clowns will _____ the children next Tuesday.

exchange	**reply**	**worship**	**city**
except	**drying**	**worse**	**cities**
excuse	**carrying**	**worst**	**circle**
piano	**foggy**	**worry**	**palace**

☆ Learn the words, then use them to do the exercises.

☆ **WORD HUNT**   Which words in the list have these smaller words inside them?

1   an   _____

2   hang   _____

3   dry   _____

4   car   _____

5   ties   _____

6   use   _____

7   ace   _____

8   ship   _____

☆ **WORD PUZZLE**   Use words from the list to complete the puzzle.

Clues down
1   answer
2   apart from
5   large towns

Clues across
2   swap
3   pardon
4   a royal residence
6   ring
7   in a more unpleasant way

☆ **WORD HUNT**   Complete these sentences with words from the list.

1   It's the _____ weather we've had for years. It was very

_____ last night and there were twelve accidents in the

_____ centre.

2   My brother is always in trouble. He's a great _____ to my parents.

giant	coin	earnest	seldom
engine	noisy	search	quite
divide	sign	French	wicked
mistake	signal	honest	selfish

☆ Learn the words, then use them to do the exercises.

☆ **OPPOSITES**   Find words in the list which mean the opposite of these words.

1 quiet   _____

2 untrustworthy _____

3 often   _____

4 multiply   _____

5 dwarf   _____

6 good   _____

7 insincere   _____

☆ **WORD PUZZLE**   Use words from the list to complete the puzzle.

Clues down
1 belonging to France
2 error

Clues across
3 machine
4 having no thought for others

☆ **EXPLANATIONS**   Complete these sentences with words from the list.

1 To provide a signature is to _____ your name.

2 To 'look for' means the same as to _____.

3 A _____ is a piece of metal money.

4 A _____ is an action or message used to send a warning.

5 _____ can mean 'completely'.

throne	area	local	cruel
choke	idea	several	Tuesday
clothes	family	second	Wednesday
owe	people	fortune	disgust

☆ Learn the words, then use them to do the exercises.

☆ **WORD HUNT**   Fill in the gaps with words from the list.

The (1) _____ (2) _____ always wear their best

(3) _____ on (4) _____ when they meet their friends at the

market.

☆ **WORD PUZZLE**   Use the word 'Wednesday' to help form nine words from the list.

be in dept

stop the breathing of

plan

large sum of money

region or district

loathing

a sixtieth of a minute

group of husband, wife and children

third day of the week

☆ **WORD HUNT**   Which words in the list have these smaller words inside them?

1 on _____

2 eve _____

3 rue _____

4 are _____

5 gust _____

6 am _____

☆ **WORD HUNT**   Complete these sentences with words from the list.

1 He won a _____ on the pools.

2 There is a large _____ of wasteland near my home.

3 I met _____ of my friends at the party.

4 The king sat on his _____.

picnic	aunt	pencil	holy
arithmetic	saucer	ocean	pony
flood	farewell	collar	navy
wooden	else	clumsy	losing

☆ Learn the words, then use them to do the exercises.

☆ **WORD PUZZLE**   Use words from the list to complete the puzzle.

Clues down

2 a nation's warships
3 awkward
4 meal eaten outside on a trip
5 calculating numbers
6 part of a garment worn round the neck
8 goodbye
10 great outpouring
13 in addition

Clues across

1 suffering loss
4 a small horse
7 small round dish
9 sister of a parent
11 sacred
12 a writing tool
14 made of wood
15 very large stretch of sea

☆ **WORD HUNT**   Complete these sentences with words from the list.

1 The opposite of 'winning' is _____.

2 The opposite of 'hello' is _____.

3 The word with the same letters as 'tuna' is _____.

4 The word with the same letters as 'canoe' is _____.

address	regret	lawyer	apply
afford	regard	gardener	allow
assist	retreat	passenger	allowed
approach	respect	drawer	clown
account	nerve	chapter	refer

☆ Learn the words, then use them to do the exercises.

☆ **WORD PUZZLE**   Use words from the list to complete the puzzle.

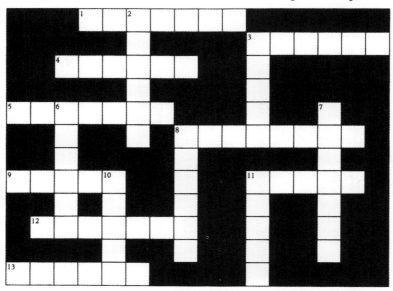

Clues down

2 a solicitor is one
3 make mention of
6 have enough money to buy something
7 report or explanation
8 help
10 courage
11 put in a request

Clues across

1 permitted
3 admiration
4 one who draws
5 part of a book
8 come nearer
9 comic entertainer
11 let
12 place where you live
13 feeling of loss

☆ **WORD MAKER**   Use words from the list to complete the words below.

1 re _ _ _ _ _ _   (to admire)

2 re _ _ _ _ _ _   (to go back)

3 re _ _ _ _   (to be sorry about)

4 _ _ _ _ er   (one who practises the law)

5 _ _ _ _ _ _ _ er   (one who tends gardens)

6 _ _ _ _ _ er   (part of a book)

direct	ankle	confess	vote
detect	sparkle	confine	devote
destroy	humble	confuse	vast
destroyed	feeble	consider	plaster
describe	steeple	convict	pastime

☆ Learn the words, then use them to do the exercises.

☆ **WORD PUZZLE**   Use words from the list to complete the puzzle.

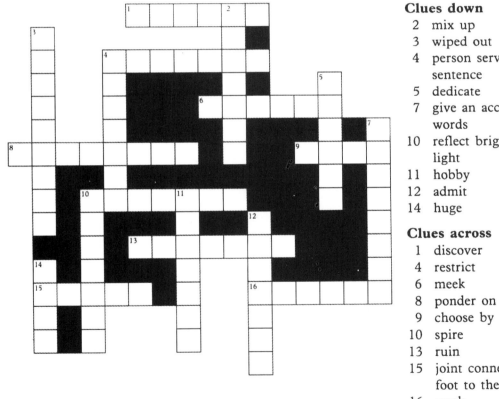

Clues down

2 mix up
3 wiped out
4 person serving a prison sentence
5 dedicate
7 give an account of in words
10 reflect bright points of light
11 hobby
12 admit
14 huge

Clues across

1 discover
4 restrict
6 meek
8 ponder on
9 choose by ballot
10 spire
13 ruin
15 joint connecting the foot to the leg
16 weak

☆ **WORD HUNT**   Complete these sentences with words from the list.

1 My father is building a new house. I helped him _____ the walls this week.

2 The policewoman helped _____ the traffic during the rush hour.

inhabit	educate	pupil	stupid
insist	education	peril	insect
invent	information	profit	sole
industry	position	credit	dose
increase	composition	splendid	whose

☆ Learn the words, then use them to do the exercises.

☆ **WORD PUZZLE**   Use the word 'information' to help make eleven words from the list.

express a strong belief

create or devise

gain

medicine to be taken

get bigger

essay

teaching given at school or college

hard work

slow witted

situation

live in

☆ **WORD HUNT**   Which words in the list have these smaller words inside them?

1 hose _____

2 mat _____

3 pup _____

4 ate _____

5 edit _____

6 lend _____

7 sect _____

8 so _____

☆ **WORD MATCH**   Find words in the list which mean the same as these words.

1 danger _____

2 marvellous _____

3 gain _____

4 foolish _____

future	dismiss	final	failure
pasture	display	finally	total
furniture	dismay	gradual	equal
manufacture	disorder	gradually	equally
departure	disappear	usually	really

☆ Learn the words, then use them to do the exercises.

☆ **OPPOSITES**   Find words in the list which mean the opposite of these words.

1 success _____

2 past   _____

3 arrival _____

4 joy   _____

5 appear _____

6 hurried   _____

7 rapidly   _____

8 tidiness _____

9 hide   _____

10 engage _____

☆ **EXPLANATIONS**   Fill the gaps in the poem with words from the list.

To (1) _____ is to make by machine or hand.

Where sheep and cattle graze is (2) _____ land.

The (3) _____ whistle ends the football game.

When things are (4) _____ they are all the same.

Much (5) _____ consists of beds and chairs.

Dividing (6) _____ gives equal shares.

(7) _____ and discharge (8) _____ mean the same.

For (9) _____, sum is just another name.

When things are said to (10) _____ unfold

They (11) _____ take some time, I'm told.

And when things happen (12) _____, it's plain,

You'll never find them happening again.

☆ **WORD HUNT**   Which words in the list have these smaller words inside them?

1 miss _____.

2 fact _____.

3 order _____.

4 play _____.

Africa	breeze	wonderful	China
America	freeze	respectful	Arctic
Canada	squeeze	awful	frozen
Atlantic	sleeve	yawn	degree
Pacific	agreeable	fully	gem

☆ Learn the words, then use them to do the exercises.

☆ **WORD PUZZLE** Use words from the list to complete the puzzle.

Clues down
1 entirely
2 turned into ice
3 university award
4 country north of USA
5 the USA
6 The world's second largest ocean
9 become very cold
12 world's most populous country
13 part of garment covering the arm
14 nasty

Clues across
5 pleasant
7 open the mouth wide and take in air when sleepy
8 light wind
10 second largest continent
11 world's largest ocean
13 press firmly
14 ocean surrounding the North Pole
15 jewel
16 marvellous
17 showing esteem or regard

hero	pickle	climate	chorus
heroes	knuckle	private	single
negro	trample	cultivate	jungle
negroes	title	decorate	article
echo	entitle	decoration	measles

☆ Learn the words, then use them to do the exercises.

☆ **WORD PUZZLE**   Use the word 'decoration' to help form ten words from the list.

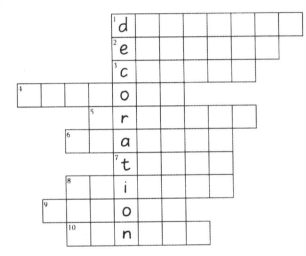

make more attractive

allow

group of singers

plural of negro

not widely known

disease common to children

name

weather conditions

plural of 'hero'

dense forest

☆ **MINI PUZZLE**   Use words from the list to complete the puzzle.

Clues down
1 a reflected sound
2 vegetables preserved in vinegar
4 black person

Clues across
3 grow
5 finger joint
6 not married
7 very brave person

☆ **WORD HUNT**   Which words in the list have these smaller words inside them?

1 ample _____   3 art _____

2 ration _____   4 mate _____

Europe	mere	fraction	telephone
Asia	merely	direction	switch
India	sincere	condition	sketch
Australia	sincerely	reduction	lantern
Russia	severe	protection	fear

☆ Learn the words, then use them to do the exercises.

☆ **WORD PUZZLE**   Use words from the list to complete the puzzle.

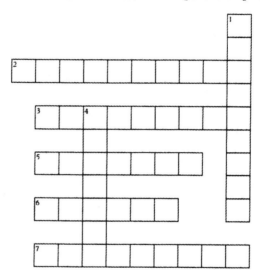

Clues down
1 genuinely
4 light with a transparent case

Clues across
2 defence
3 device which transmits and receives speech
5 genuine
6 a rapid drawing
7 state of health

☆ **WORD HUNT**   Fill in the gaps with words from the list.

(1) _____ is the smallest continent and largest island in the world.

(2) _____, the next smallest continent, is only a (3) _____ of the size of (4) _____, the largest.

☆ **WORD HUNT**   Which words from the list have these smaller words inside them?

1 red _____

2 eve _____

3 rely _____

4 witch _____

5 direct _____

terrible	saddle	northern	limb
horrible	struggle	southern	modern
possible	puzzle	eastern	modest
impossible	latter	western	screw
improve	parrot	shepherd	nephew

☆ Learn the words, then use them to do the exercises.

☆ **WORD HUNT**   Fill in the gaps with words from the list.

The Opposite Parrot

There was once an old (1) _____ whose only relative was his young

(2) _____. They had little money so it was a (3) _____ to make

ends meet. One day the boy caught a (4) _____. "I will teach it to speak,"

the boy said. But whatever the boy said, the bird always said the opposite.

"Say northern," the boy said.

"(5) _____," said the bird.

"Say possible," the boy said.

"(6) _____," said the bird.

"Say eastern," the boy said.

"(7) _____," said the bird.

"Say ancient," said the boy.

"(8) _____," said the bird.

"Say boastful," said the boy.

"(9) _____," said the bird.

The boy said, "This is (10) _____. You will have to

(11) _____, you (12) _____ bird. It must be

(13) _____ for you to learn." But the bird never did.

It has been a (14) _____ to the boy ever since.

☆ **WORD HUNT**   Complete these sentences with words from the list.

1 The word _____ has a silent 'b'.

2 The opposite of 'southern' is _____.

3 The word _____ has 'sad' inside it.

double	dispute	regular	flourish
trouble	displease	popular	prey
couple	disobey	particular	victim
courage	district	singular	cigar
encourage	disturb	vinegar	calendar

☆ Learn the words, then use them to do the exercises.

☆ **WORD PUZZLE**   Use the word 'particular' to help form ten words from the list.

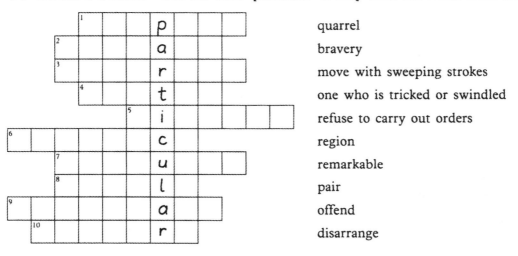

quarrel

bravery

move with sweeping strokes

one who is tricked or swindled

refuse to carry out orders

region

remarkable

pair

offend

disarrange

☆ **WORD HUNT**   Complete these sentences with words from the list.

1   Your _____ is a person who closely resembles you.

2   _____ attenders at school are rarely absent.

3   Angling is a _____ pastime in Britain.

4   When you _____ people you give them lots of help.

5   An eagle is a bird of _____.

6   He causes _____ wherever he goes.

☆ **WORD MAKER**   Use words from the list to complete the words below.

1   _ _ _ _ _ ar   (someone who is liked is this)

2   _ _ _ _ _ _ ar   (a list of days, weeks and months)

3   _ _ _ _ _ ar   (usual or customary)

4   _ _ _ _ _ _ _ _ ar (special)

5   _ _ _ _ _ ar   (a sour liquid)

erect	canal	mistress	trial
elect	capital	misfortune	loyal
election	rural	mischief	royal
electric	mortal	handkerchief	rascal
halt	funeral	handsome	musical

☆ Learn the words, then use them to do the exercises.

☆ **WORD PUZZLE**   Use words from the list to complete the puzzle.

Clues down

1 in the country
2 woman in charge
3 manmade waterway
5 powered by electricity
6 bad luck
7 choice by vote
8 deadly
9 good looking

Clues across

4 talented in music
7 choose by voting
8 naughtiness
10 chief city of a country
11 befitting a king or queen
12 small square of material for
    wiping the nose

☆ **WORD HUNT**   Complete these sentences with words from the list.

1 I had to _____ at the traffic lights.

2 The _____ in court took four days.

3 Two hundred mourners attended the _____.

4 The house took nine months to _____.

5 He is a _____ supporter of that football team.

6 The little _____ is always in mischief.

detain	procure	revive	secret
retain	endure	revenge	select
complain	feature	reverse	request
bargain	torture	resolve	require
waist	secure	resemble	inquire

☆ Learn the words, then use them to do the exercises.

☆ **WORD PUZZLE**   Use the word 'resemble' to help form eight words from the list.

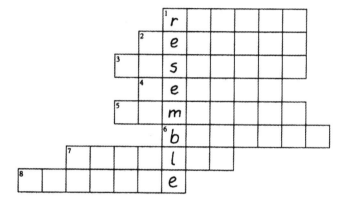

bring back to life

vengeance

look like

kept from others

grumble

something bought cheaply

decide firmly

ask

☆ **MINI PUZZLE**   Use words from the list to complete the puzzle.

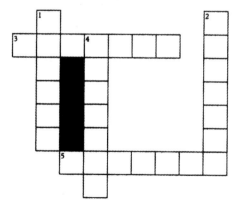

Clues down
1 hold back
2 need
4 cause great pain

Clues across
3 main film at a cinema
5 obtain

☆ **WORD HUNT**   Which words in the list have these smaller words inside them?

1 quest _____   4 is _____

2 elect _____   5 verse _____

3 end _____

ordinary	image	exact	exist
library	imagine	exactly	example
January	imagination	expand	bury
February	examine	extract	buried
enemy	examination	exercise	ivy

☆ Learn the words, then use them to do the exercises.

☆ **WORD HUNT**   Which words in the list have these smaller words inside them?

1 din _____   5 tract _____

2 ample _____   6 pan _____

3 age _____   7 is _____

4 mine _____

☆ **WORD HUNT**   Fill in the gaps with words from the list.

The Siege

In December, what I had long feared in my (1) _____ now became real.

For days (2) _____ guns were heard in the distance. Then

(3) _____ one week after Christmas Day the siege of our town began. The

date was (4) _____ 1st. Four or five weeks later, (5) _____ 1st

to be (6) _____, the (7) _____ was over. A brief

(8) _____ revealed that all the public buildings, except the

(9) _____ had been destroyed. You can (10) _____ how terrible

I felt in those dreadful times.

☆ **EXPLANATIONS**   Complete these sentences with words from the list.

1 _____ is a kind of creeper.

2 'To put something underground' is to _____ it.

3 If you say 'someone _____ themselves in their books', you mean they

gave all their attention to them.

☆ **WORD MAKER**   Use words from the list to complete the words below.

1 ex_____ (to inspect)   3 ex___ (to have life)

2 ex_____ (precisely)   4 ex____ (to make larger)

loan	preserve	fortunate	compose
coax	prepare	unfortunate	advise
oath	compare	moderate	promise
active	beware	estimate	glimpse
action	betray	happiness	sense

☆ Learn the words, then use them to do the exercises.

☆ **WORD PUZZLE**   Use the word 'fortunate' to help form nine words from the list.

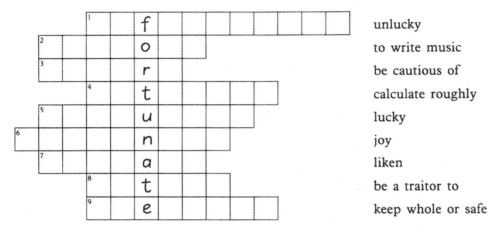

1. unlucky
2. to write music
3. be cautious of
4. calculate roughly
5. lucky
6. joy
7. liken
8. be a traitor to
9. keep whole or safe

☆ **MINI PUZZLE**   Use words from the list to complete the puzzle.

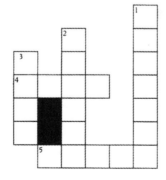

Clues down
1 brief view
2 busy
3 to lend

Clues across
4 solemn promise
5 awareness

☆ **WORD MATCH**   Find words in the list which mean the same as these words.

1 counsel _____   4 assure _____

2 temperate _____   5 persuade _____

3 deed _____   6 get ready _____

wrestle	beggar	produce	chimney
wrist	cellar	promote	turkey
written	pillar	progress	tune
gentleman	grammar	possess	tube
heathen	burglar	entire	costume

☆ Learn the words, then use them to do the exercises.

☆ **WORD HUNT**   Which words in the list have these smaller words inside them?

1 rest _____

2 is _____

3 ten _____

4 men _____

5 eat _____

6 him _____

7 beg _____

8 ill _____

9 ram _____

10 key _____

11 rod _____

12 tub _____

13 tire _____

14 cost _____

15 cell _____

☆ **MINI PUZZLE**   Use words from the list to complete the puzzle.

Clues down
1 housebreaker
2 raise to a higher rank
3 own

Clues across
4 melody
5 movement forward

☆ **WORD MATCH**   Find words in the list which mean the same as these words.

1 manufacture _____

2 robber _____

3 basement _____

4 grapple _____

5 whole _____

6 own _____

discontent	grocer	mention	elbow
represent	groceries	attention	growth
evident	tempt	situation	speech
frequent	attempt	invitation	graze
accident	temptation	truly	naked

☆ Learn the words, then use them to do the exercises.

☆ **WORD PUZZLE**   Use words from the list to complete the puzzle.

Clues down

2 an offer
4 happening very
    often
6 a talk
7 special care

8 entice
9 provisions
12 a dealer in
    foodstuffs

Clues across

1 unforeseen event
3 obvious
5 try
6 place
10 in truth

11 speak about briefly
13 enticement
14 dissatisfaction
15 without clothes
16 an increase in size

☆ **WORD HUNT**   Complete these sentences with words from the list.

1 The cattle are allowed to _____ in the meadow.

2 I hit my _____ on the table and hurt my funny bone.

accept	honour	labour	sober
according	harbour	devour	basin
plunge	habit	justice	cabin
population	pigeon	practice	rapid
satin	gulf	service	payment

☆ Learn the words, then use them to do the exercises.

☆ **WORD PUZZLE**   Use the word 'population' to help form ten words from the list.

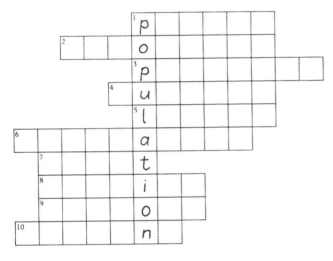

a leap or dive into water

dependent on

repeating an activity to gain skill

fairness

work

all the persons of a country

usual custom

an act of help

a sheltered port

fee

☆ **MINI PUZZLE**   Use words from the list to complete the puzzle.

Clues down
1 open container for liquids
2 eat
4 large deep bay
5 swift

Clues across
3 receive
6 great respect
7 small, simple dwelling hut

☆ **WORD HUNT**   Which words in the list have these smaller words inside them?

1 be _____

2 pig _____

3 sat _____

4 act _____

excite	construct	explore	expel
exciting	contribute	exploration	angry
excellent	consume	explanation	envy
exclaim	confirm	style	idea
exclaimed	contrast	pavement	oblige

☆ Learn the words, then use them to do the exercises.

☆ **WORD HUNT**   Which words in the list have these smaller words inside them?

1 lent _____
2 men _____
3 as _____
4 firm _____
5 claimed _____

6 sum _____
7 lore _____
8 but _____
9 plan _____
10 rat _____

☆ **WORD HUNT**   Complete these sentences with words from the list.

1 The word with the same letters as 'rangy' is _____.
2 The word which means to 'cry out' is _____.
3 The word with the letter 'i' twice is _____.
4 The word which means 'jealousy' is _____.
5 The word with the same letters as 'aide' is _____.
6 The word which means 'build' is _____.

☆ **STEP WORDS**   Use words from the list to complete the puzzle.

Clues down
  2 arouse strong feelings
  4 drive out

Clues across
  1 do a favour to
  3 examine closely

height	junior	gospel	parcel
either	language	compel	course
neither	monument	chapel	veil
reign	department	jewel	vein
foreign	swear	bushel	neighbour

☆ Learn the words, then use them to do the exercises.

☆ **WORD PUZZLE**   Use words from the list to complete the puzzle.

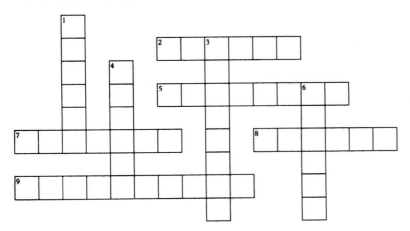

Clues down

1 one or the other
3 building to honour a great person
4 lower in rank
6 the story of Christ's life

Clues across

2 force
5 communication by speech
7 coming from another country
8 eight gallon measure
9 branch of a large concern

☆ **WORD MAKER**   Use words from the list to complete the words below.

1 _ei_   (used to hide face)

2 _ei_   (vessel to carry blood)

3 _ei__   (period of rule)

4 _ei____   (not one or other)

5 _ei_____   (person living next door)

☆ **MINI PUZZLE**   Use the word 'parcel' to help form six words from the list.

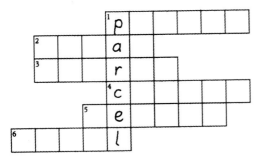

wrapped goods

take an oath

direction

place of worship

measure from base to top

gem

Answers

2 WORD PUZZLE **Clues down** (2) nicely
(3) laugh (5) weakness (6) motor (7) lately
(8) laughter (9) victory (10) likely (11) safely
Clues across (1) linger (4) likeness (7) laughed
(8) lovely (12) inform (13) lonely (14) visitor
WORD HUNT (1) lonely (2) nicely (3) inform
(4) lately
WORD MAKER (1) lonely (2) likely (3) lovely
(4) lately

3 OPPOSITES (1) distant (2) important
(3) constant (4) admire (5) arrive (6) ashamed
(7) admit
WORD PUZZLE (1) advice (2) amuse
(3) empire (4) though (5) through (6) nature
(7) merchant (8) adventure (9) servant
WORD HUNT (1) servant (2) adventure
(3) amuse (4) distant (5) ashamed (6) adventure
(7) constant

4 WORD HUNT (1) sailor (2) tailor (3) holiday
(4) object (5) equator (6) rough (7) rainy
(8) evening (9) tough (10) enough (11) railway
(12) Rocky (13) daily (14) event (15) robin

5 WORD HUNT (1) carrot (2) village
(3) sparrow (4) scatter (5) cabbage (6) swallow
(7) valleys (8) ragged (9) thought
WORD PUZZLE (1) bought (2) brass
(3) gallop (4) fought (5) village (6) thought
(7) ought
EXPLANATIONS (1) brought (2) scatter
(3) fought (4) valley
WORD HUNT (1) ragged (2) brass (3) gallop

6 WORD PUZZLE **Clues down** (1) against
(2) hasty (4) nasty (5) parish (6) fancy
(9) banish (11) ugly
Clues across (1) across (3) alone (7) among
(8) shady (10) study (12) vanish (13) Welsh
(14) polish
WORD MATCH (1) vanish (2) banish
(3) perish (4) hasty (5) ugly (6) among
OPPOSITES (1) hasty (2) against (3) vanish
(4) fancy

7 WORD HUNT (1) famous (2) welcome
(3) lawn (4) dangerous (5) faithfully (6) laid
WORD PUZZLE (1) unable (2) until (3) lays
(4) beauty (5) laying (6) welcome
OPPOSITES (1) dawn (2) beautiful (3) thankful
(4) careful (5) carefully (6) dangerous
WORD MATCH (1) beautiful (2) famous
(3) faithfully

8 WORD MAKER (1) noble (2) kindle
(3) grumble (4) tremble

WORD HUNT (1) protect (2) monster
(3) glance (4) thimble (5) bundle (6) scramble
(7) kindle (8) stumble (9) advance (10) France
(11) grumble (12) distance
WORD PUZZLE **Clues down** (1) stumble
(2) glance (3) advance (4) tremble (6) thimble
(8) bough
Clues across (5) monster (7) France (9) noble
(10) plough

9 WORD PUZZLE **Clues down** (1) bucket
(2) tight (3) terror (5) liberty (6) mutton
(7) mighty (10) cotton (12) shrub
Clues across (2) trumpet (4) slight (8) error
(9) delight (10) correct (11) Scottish (13) ribbon
(14) blossom
OPPOSITES (1) tight (2) mighty (3) correct
(4) liberty (5) slight
WORD MATCH (1) delight (2) liberty
(3) terror (4) error

10 WORD PUZZLE (1) dislike (2) discuss
(3) discover (4) stalk (5) razor (6) gaze
(7) distinct (8) disgrace
WORD MAKER (1) salt (2) chalk (3) alter
(4) blaze (5) prize (6) size
OPPOSITES (1) lazy (2) discover (3) distress
(4) distinct

11 WORD PUZZLE **Clues down** (1) rubber
(3) bullet (4) station (6) quarrel (7) nation
(8) dictation (9) companion (10) quarter
(13) motion
Clues across (2) publish (5) barrel (6) question
(11) quart (12) company (15) astonish
WORD HUNT (1) appear (2) astonish (3) bullet

12 WORD HUNT (1) occupy (2) hollow
(3) combine (4) coffee (5) piece (6) ourselves
WORD PUZZLE **Clues down** (2) occurred
(3) wharf (5) wharves (6) occupy (7) niece
(8) grieve (12) belief
Clues across (1) hollow (4) horrid (6) occur
(9) ourselves (10) piece (11) combine
(13) believe (14) forgotten

13 WORD HUNT (1) officer (2) office (3) knit
(4) different (5) skirt (6) bonnet (7) mirror
(8) knitting
WORD MAKER (1) caught (2) taught
(3) daughter (4) naughty (5) stir (6) skirt
(7) mirror
WORD HUNT (1) bonnet (2) stirred (3) skill
(4) different (5) knight

14 WORD PUZZLE **Clues down** (1) foe
(2) steadily (3) butcher (4) statue (7) shilling
(10) tomato (12) poetry (13) weary

Clues across (5) continue (6) potato (8) thread
(9) instead (11) value (14) potatoes (15) wearily
WORD HUNT (1) tomatoes (2) Statue
(3) thread

15 WORD HUNT (1) tiger (2) cunning
(3) treasure (4) tunnel (5) muddy (6) reward
(7) suppose (8) pleasure (9) pleasant (10) shoe
(11) throat (12) groan (13) defeat (14) coach
(15) measure (16) toast
WORD MATCH (1) cunning (2) pleasure
(3) defeat (4) pleasant

16 WORD HUNT (1) prettier, prettiest
(2) wedding (3) herring (4) journey (5) dwelling
(6) beginning (7) swept (8) obey, obeyed
(9) group (10) youth
WORD PUZZLE (1) obey (2) vessel (3) group
(4) prettier (5) dwelling (6) wedding (7) prettiest
(8) journey (9) herring
WORD HUNT (1) wound (2) calm (3) crept

17 STEP WORDS Clues down (2) demand
(4) delay
Clues across (1) beyond (3) depend
WORD MAKER (1) breath (2) leather
(3) weather (4) feather (5) healthy (6) wealthy
EXPLANATIONS (1) recall (2) shiver
(3) result (4) health (5) meant

18 WORD PUZZLE Clues down (1) queer
(2) steer (4) greedy (5) powder (7) screen
(8) drowned (9) aim (10) petrol
Clues across (3) engage (6) praise (8) deer
(11) freedom (12) dairy (13) drown (14) fleet
(15) claim
WORD MATCH (1) screen (2) queer
(3) freedom (4) engage (5) greedy (6) aim

19 WORD PUZZLE (1) British (2) Irish
(3) season (4) guilty (5) reason (6) crimson
(7) board
WORD HUNT (1) Briton (2) warn (3) Ireland
(4) crimson (5) metal (6) board (7) mental
(8) Briton, iron
WORD MAKER (1) medal (2) mental (3) guide
(4) guest (5) season (6) crimson (7) iron

20 WORD PUZZLE Clues down (1) deserve
(2) rare (3) restore (4) vase (7) refuse (9) retire
(10) October (13) behave
Clues across (1) desire (3) relate (5) square
(6) Germany (8) bravery (11) herd
(12) December (14) bathe
WORD HUNT (1) bravery (2) herd (3) retire

21 WORD PUZZLE Clues down (1) wreck
(2) hedge (3) judge (6) check

Clues across (4) attend (5) attack (7) edge
(8) badge
OPPOSITES (1) wrong (2) attack (3) stout
(4) sour
WORD HUNT (1) bridge (2) trout (3) flour
(4) lodge (5) sword

22 MINI PUZZLE Clues down (1) banana
(2) whom (3) score (4) memory
Clues across (1) bowl (5) orange (6) wore
(7) factory
WORD MAKER (1) pavement (2) basement
(3) suit (4) fruit
WORD HUNT (1) member (2) remember
(3) weather (4) remembered

23 WORD PUZZLE Clues down (1) huge
(2) truth (3) scripture (5) duty (6) creature
(7) figure
Clues across (3) shoulder (4) pour
(5) dumb (6) court (8) using (9) during
WORD HUNT (1) dumb (2) eight (3) weigh
(4) during (5) weight (6) entertain

24 WORD HUNT (1) piano (2) exchange
(3) drying (4) carrying (5) cities (6) excuse
(7) palace (8) worship
WORD PUZZLE Clues down (1) reply
(2) except (5) cities
Clues across (2) exchange (3) excuse (4) palace
(6) circle (7) worse
WORD HUNT (1) worst, foggy, city (2) worry

25 OPPOSITES (1) noisy (2) honest (3) seldom
(4) divide (5) giant (6) wicked (7) earnest
WORD PUZZLE Clues down (1) French
(2) mistake
Clues across (3) engine (4) selfish
EXPLANATIONS (1) sign (2) search (3) coin
(4) signal (5) Quite

26 WORD HUNT (1) local (2) people (3) clothes
(4) Wednesday/Tuesday
WORD PUZZLE (1) owe (2) choke (3) idea
(4) fortune (5) area (6) disgust (7) second
(8) family (9) Tuesday
WORD HUNT (1) second, throne (2) several
(3) cruel (4) area (5) disgust (6) family
WORD HUNT (1) fortune (2) area (3) several
(4) throne

27 WORD PUZZLE Clues down (2) navy
(3) clumsy (4) picnic (5) arithmetic (6) collar
(8) farewell (10) flood (13) else
Clues across (1) losing (4) pony (7) saucer
(9) aunt (11) holy (12) pencil (14) wooden
(15) ocean
WORD HUNT (1) losing (2) farewell (3) aunt
(4) ocean

28 WORD PUZZLE **Clues down** (2) lawyer
(3) refer (6) afford (7) account (8) assist
(10) nerve (11) apply
Clues across (1) allowed (3) regard (4) drawer
(5) chapter (8) approach (9) clown
(12) address (13) regret
WORD MAKER (1) respect (2) retreat
(3) regret (4) lawyer (5) gardener (6) chapter

29 WORD PUZZLE **Clues down** (2) confuse
(3) destroyed (4) convict (5) devote (7) describe
(10) sparkle (11) pastime (12) confess (14) vast
Clues across (1) detect (4) confine (6) humble
(8) consider (9) vote (10) steeple (13) destroy
(15) ankle (16) feeble
WORD HUNT (1) plaster (2) direct

30 WORD PUZZLE (1) insist (2) invent
(3) profit (4) dose (5) increase (6) composition
(7) education (8) industry (9) stupid
(10) position (11) inhabit
WORD HUNT (1) whose (2) information
(3) pupil (4) educate (5) credit (6) splendid
(7) insect (8) sole
WORD MATCH (1) peril (2) splendid
(3) profit (4) stupid

31 OPPOSITES (1) failure (2) future
(3) departure (4) dismay (5) disappear
(6) gradual (7) gradually (8) disorder (9) display
(10) dismiss
EXPLANATIONS (1) manufacture (2) pasture
(3) final (4) equal (5) furniture (6) equally
(7) dismiss (8) really (9) total (10) gradually
(11) usually (12) finally
WORD HUNT (1) dismiss (2) manufacture
(3) disorder (4) display

32 WORD PUZZLE **Clues down** (1) fully
(2) frozen (3) degree (4) Canada (5) America
(6) Atlantic (9) freeze (12) China (13) sleeve
(14) awful
Clues across (5) agreeable (7) yawn (8) breeze
(10) Africa (11) Pacific (13) squeeze (14) Arctic
(15) gem (16) wonderful (17) respectful

33 WORD PUZZLE (1) decorate (2) entitle
(3) chorus (4) negroes (5) private (6) measles
(7) title (8) climate (9) heroes (10) jungle
MINI PUZZLE **Clues down** (1) echo
(2) pickle (4) negro
Clues across (3) cultivate (5) knuckle
(6) single (7) hero
WORD HUNT (1) trample (2) decoration
(3) article (4) climate

34 WORD PUZZLE **Clues down** (1) sincerely
(4) lantern

Clues across (2) protection (3) telephone
(5) sincere (6) sketch (7) condition
WORD HUNT (1) Australia (2) Europe
(3) fraction (4) Asia
WORD HUNT (1) reduction (2) severe
(3) merely (4) switch (5) direction

35 WORD HUNT (1) shepherd (2) nephew
(3) struggle (4) parrot (5) Southern
(6) Impossible (7) Western (8) Modern
(9) Modest (10) terrible (11) improve
(12) horrible (13) possible (14) puzzle
WORD HUNT (1) limb (2) Northern
(3) saddle

36 WORD PUZZLE (1) dispute (2) courage
(3) flourish (4) victim (5) disobey (6) district
(7) singular (8) couple (9) displease (10) disturb
WORD HUNT (1) double (2) Regular
(3) popular (4) encourage (5) prey (6) trouble
WORD MAKER (1) popular (2) calendar
(3) regular (4) particular (5) vinegar

37 WORD PUZZLE **Clues down** (1) rural
(2) mistress (3) canal (5) electric (6) misfortune
(7) election (8) mortal (9) handsome
Clues across (4) musical (7) elect (8) mischief
(10) capital (11) royal (12) handkerchief
WORD HUNT (1) halt (2) trial (3) funeral
(4) erect (5) loyal (6) rascal

38 WORD PUZZLE (1) revive (2) revenge
(3) resemble (4) secret (5) complain (6) bargain
(7) resolve (8) inquire
MINI PUZZLE **Clues down** (1) retain
(2) require (4) torture
Clues across (3) feature (5) procure
WORD HUNT (1) request (2) select (3) endure
(4) waist (5) reverse

39 WORD HUNT (1) ordinary (2) example (3) image
(4) examine (5) extract (6) expand (7) exist, exercise
WORD HUNT (1) imagination (2) enemy
(3) exactly (4) January (5) February (6) exact
(7) exercise (8) examination (9) library
(10) imagine
EXPLANATIONS (1) Ivy (2) bury (3) buried
WORD MAKER (1) examine (2) exactly
(3) exist (4) expand

40 WORD HUNT (1) unfortunate (2) compose
(3) beware (4) estimate (5) fortunate
(6) happiness (7) compare (8) betray (9) preserve
MINI PUZZLE **Clues down** (1) glimpse
(2) active (3) loan
Clues across (4) oath (5) sense
WORD MATCH (1) advise (2) moderate
(3) action (4) promise (5) coax (6) prepare